About Pfeiffer

Pfeiffer serves the professional development and hands-on resource needs of training and human resource practitioners and gives them products to do their jobs better. We deliver proven ideas and solutions from experts in HR development and HR management, and we offer effective and customizable tools to improve workplace performance. From novice to seasoned professional, Pfeiffer is the source you can trust to make yourself and your organization more successful.

 **Essential Knowledge** Pfeiffer produces insightful, practical, and comprehensive materials on topics that matter the most to training and HR professionals. Our Essential Knowledge resources translate the expertise of seasoned professionals into practical, how-to guidance on critical workplace issues and problems. These resources are supported by case studies, worksheets, and job aids and are frequently supplemented with CD-ROMs, websites, and other means of making the content easier to read, understand, and use.

Essential Tools Pfeiffer's Essential Tools resources save time and expense by offering proven, ready-to-use materials—including exercises, activities, games, instruments, and assessments—for use during a training or team-learning event. These resources are frequently offered in looseleaf or CD-ROM format to facilitate copying and customization of the material.

Pfeiffer also recognizes the remarkable power of new technologies in expanding the reach and effectiveness of training. While e-hype has often created whizbang solutions in search of a problem, we are dedicated to bringing convenience and enhancements to proven training solutions. All our e-tools comply with rigorous functionality standards. The most appropriate technology wrapped around essential content yields the perfect solution for today's on-the-go trainers and human resource professionals.

Pfeiffer
www.pfeiffer.com

Essential resources for training and HR professionals

T0087591

Trouble on the Inca Trail

Participant's Workbook

Lorraine L. Ukens

Pfeiffer

A Wiley Imprint

www.pfeiffer.com

Published by Pfeiffer
An Imprint of Wiley
989 Market Street, San Francisco, CA 94103-1741   www.pfeiffer.com

For additional copies/bulk purchases of this book in the U.S. please contact 800-274-4434.
Pfeiffer books and products are available through most bookstores. To contact Pfeiffer directly call our Customer Care Department within the U.S. at 800-274-4434, outside the U.S. at 317-572-3985 or fax 317-572-4002 or www.pfeiffer.com.
Pfeiffer also publishes its books in a variety of electronic formats. Some content that appears in print may not be available in electronic books.

ISBN: 0-7879-7603-2

Acquiring Editor: Martin Delahoussaye
Director of Development: Kathleen Dolan Davies
Developmental Editor: Susan Rachmeler
Editor: Rebecca Taff
Senior Production Editor: Dawn Kilgore
Marketing Manager: Jeanenne Ray
Manufacturing Supervisor: Bill Matherly

Printed in the United States of America

Printing 10   9   8   7

Contents

Iquitos

Amazon

Pacaya-
Samiria
National
Reserve

Pucallpa

LIMA

Machu
Picchu

Paucarcancha

Cusco

Nazca

Lake
Titicaca

Trouble on the Inca Trail

THE SITUATION

You and a small group of friends are embarking on an extended trek across Peru that will follow along the famous Inca Trail. In ancient times, the Trail was used to connect all four corners of the Incan Empire. Your route will begin in Nazca, head east to Cusco, and then move north to Iquitos. The journey will take you through three diverse ecological zones until your travels end at the isolated and primitive Pacaya-Samiria National Reserve, known to natives as the "jungle of mirrors." You will be traversing the desolate, dry Pacific coastal desert in the west; move across the centrally located, sometimes snow-capped Andes Mountains; and finally move into the lush tropical rainforest region of the Amazon Basin in northeastern Peru.

The famous Inca Trail has a well-earned reputation for the variety of flora and fauna encountered, with landscapes that run up the pass at 4,000 meters above sea level and then along a path overwhelmed by steamy jungle vegetation. Along the way, you will walk past mysterious archaeological sites half-hidden in thick undergrowth, including Machu Picchu, the "Lost City of the Incas," which is one of the world's most breathtaking sites. You will be one of the thousands who flock from all over the world to have a first-hand experience of the same trail that the Incas walked more than five hundred years ago.

Although the best time to walk the Inca Trail is from May to October, the group has decided to make its trip during April before the peak tourist season begins. However, you realize that this is a time when fewer people travel the Trail and that any problems may isolate you in any of the various locations you encounter. Most of the trail is fairly safe, but it should not be taken lightly. Some stretches wind past high cliffs, and it is easy to get lost or fall off the trail. You have made your preparations, and now it is time for the expedition to begin.

YOUR TASK

Do not communicate with anyone else. Read the predicaments that follow, choose the best answer from the three alternatives provided in each case, and write the letter (a, b, or c) that corresponds to your answer in the space provided under the heading "Your Answer." You will have fifteen minutes to complete the task, and the facilitator will give you a two-minute warning before time expires.

Predicament	*Your Answer*	*Group's Answer*	*Correct Answer*

1. You start your trip in the dry coastal desert region of Nazca, and as your proceed, the day becomes dry and extremely hot. You have with you a full canteen of water (approximately one liter) that must last you until you reach Cusco two days from now. You decide to:

    a. drink as much water as you think you need before you begin to feel thirsty.

    b. ration the water, allowing for only one cup each day.

    c. not have any water until you stop for the night, and then drink what you feel you need.

2. As the sweltering day drags on, you begin to suffer from cramps, dizziness, and profuse sweating. You recognize these symptoms as heat exhaustion and know that in order to prevent further distress you need to:

    a. move about very slowly until the symptoms subside.

    b. eat a chocolate bar.

    c. drink some lightly salted water.

3. Two days later you arrive in Cusco and spend the night preparing for your expedition. After a restful night, early the next morning you make your way toward the archaeological ruins of Paucarcancha. When you reach them later that afternoon, you begin your explorations, but realize that there is definite danger in encountering snakes that inhabit the building remnants and natural outcroppings of the area. The best way to avoid snakes and potential harm is to:

    a. make a lot of noise.

    b. walk softly and quietly.

    c. wait until early evening.

4. You have settled into camp for the night, and you are preparing a meal for the evening. As you are removing a pot from the campfire, you realize that you are too close to the flame and your shirt sleeve has ignited. You quickly put out the fire, but you have suffered a rather severe burn. The best way to treat the burn and keep it from becoming infected is to:

   _____ _____ _____

a. apply antiseptic ointment.

b. remove any adhered particles of charred clothing.

c. soak your arm in the nearby mountain stream.

5. It is soon morning and you have survived the night without further difficulty. After several hours of walking inland, you find yourself at the foot of the Andes Mountains. From here the trail ascends steeply; you must now begin your route up on the mossy, slippery rock. The safest approach would be to:

   _____ _____ _____

a. keep your boots on for the ascent.

b. proceed with only your socks on.

c. go up the rocks in your bare feet.

6. You have reached the summit and the air is crisp and clear. You realize that you are about to spend your first evening in the mountains, and you decide to go out on a brief foraging trip. As you try to make your way back to the campsite, your flashlight starts to glow dimly. Your surroundings are unfamiliar to you and the pitch dark of a moonless night is descending quickly. You should: _____ _____ _____

    a. put the batteries under your armpits to warm them for a while and then replace them in the flashlight.

    b. alternate the process of shining your light for a few seconds to get the scene in mind and then moving carefully forward into the darkness for a while.

    c. head back at once, clicking the light off and on, and hoping the flashlight will glow enough for you to make out landmarks.

7. You awaken refreshed after a good night's rest. After walking along the main trail most of the day, you decide to try to locate a more scenic, yet less-traveled alternate route. You have enjoyed the sights and now start to head back toward the central trail. You realize that you have gone farther than anticipated, and you still have not located the trail after the sun dips below the horizon. Night begins to fall and your flashlight batteries finally wear down completely. You know that you should be heading east, but you are unsure of your current direction. You decide to rely on your knowledge of celestial navigation by observing the: _____ _____ _____

    a. North Star.

    b. Southern Cross.

    c. moon.

8. You feel relieved when you find your way back to
   camp as the wind suddenly begins to howl. You
   quickly retreat to your tent for the night and pull the
   flap tightly closed. You have a small stove burning
   inside to keep you warm. However, you need to
   keep a close eye on it because there is a danger of
   carbon monoxide if the flame begins to glow: _____ _____ _____

   a. red.

   b. yellow.

   c. blue.

9. The next morning is bright and clear as you reach
   the ancient ruins of Machu Picchu. After spending
   several hours visiting the Inca site, you begin the
   descent from the mountainous area on your way
   toward Iquitos near the Amazon River. Before making camp for the evening, you must cross a stream
   that is about waist deep and has a strong current. To
   get safely across, you should face: _____ _____ _____

   a. upstream.

   b. downstream.

   c. across the stream.

10. After several days, your journey has finally taken
   you into the tropical rainforest region of the Amazon
   Basin. After walking all day, you are tired and
   begin to think about preparing for your first night in
   the jungle. The most important thing now is to set
   up camp: _____ _____ _____

   a. near a source of water.

   b. at the base of a large tree for protection.

   c. no later than 4:00 in the afternoon.

11. The following day takes you deeper into the jungle, and you see a variety of plants and birds that you have never seen before. You come to a murky stream that must be crossed in order to proceed through an area of less dense vegetation. As you emerge from the water, you look down to see that a leech has attached itself to your leg. The best way to remove the leech is to: _____ _____ _____

a. apply iodine.

b. cover it with coffee grounds.

c. pull it off with a quick and firm motion.

12. You continue walking for most of the day and make it to the edges of the Reserve. You are reaching the last part of your trek when you step into some densely covered undergrowth. You feel a soft ooze begin to suck at your ankles, and then suddenly you find yourself standing in sand up to your knees. You realize it is quicksand! You should: _____ _____ _____

a. fall flat on your back and float.

b. try to swim out.

c. stand absolutely still.

Individual Score = _____

Average Individual Score = _____

Total Group Score = _____

GUIDELINES FOR REACHING CONSENSUS

Your group will supply a number of resources that each member lacked when you worked independently on the task. Enter into the group task with a commitment to use these resources and arrive at the best possible solutions. Shoulder your share of the responsibility for the group's success, and discuss the task and process openly and candidly. Use flexible patterns of communication so that all members of your group will be able to participate equally and will feel free to speak up when they have a need to do so. Minority opinions should be encouraged; not only will this increase participation, but it could supply information or logic that previously was missing.

The following guidelines will help during the decision-making process:

1. *Think through your own ideas* as well as you can before meeting with the group (but realize that others may know information that you do not).

2. *Express your own opinions and explain yourself fully*, so that the rest of the group has the benefit of all members' thinking.

3. *Listen to the opinions and feelings of all other group members* and be ready to modify your own position on the basis of logic and understanding.

4. *Avoid arguing for your own position* in order to "win" as an individual; what is "right" is the best collective judgment of the group as a whole.

5. *View disagreements or conflict as helping to clarify the issue*, rather than as hindering the process. Do not "give in" if you still have serious reservations about an issue; instead, work toward resolution.

6. *Recognize that tension-reducing behaviors, such as laughing or kidding, can be useful*, as long as meaningful conflict is not smoothed over prematurely.

7. *Refrain from conflict-reducing techniques*, such as voting, averaging, trading, compromising, or giving in to keep the peace.

8. *Monitor interactions among people* as the group attempts to complete its work and initiate discussions of what really is going on.

9. *Do not assume that an answer is correct* just because there is agreement initially. Discuss the reasons for the answer and explore all possibilities.

GROUP'S TASK

This task is similar to the task you performed individually, but it will be shared by your whole group. Assume that the entire group faces each predicament. The group task will be an exercise in group decision making, and your group will employ the group-consensus method in reaching its decisions. In many cases, a consensus will be difficult to reach. Therefore, not every answer may meet with everyone's *complete* approval, but each answer must be one that every member is willing to accept. When a consensus decision has been reached for each predicament, write the letter (a, b, or c) that corresponds to the answer your group selected in the space provided under the heading "Group's Answer." Leave the "Correct Answer" space blank until the facilitator gives you scoring instructions. You will have approximately one-half hour for the group task.

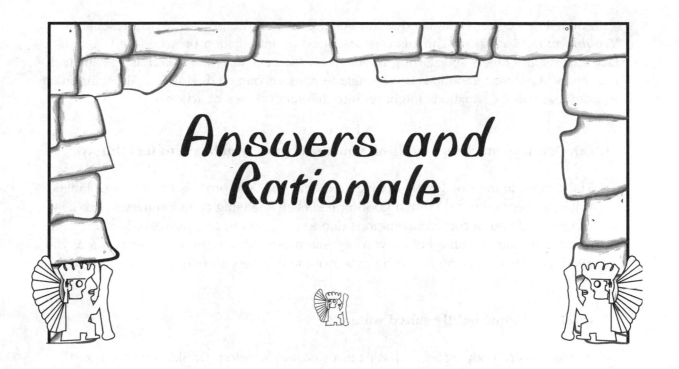

Answers and
Rationale

Following are the recommended answers for each of the predicaments presented in *Trouble on the Inca Trail*. The answers are based on information provided by U.S. military experts and others specializing in general wilderness survival as well as specific techniques for the desert, mountain, and jungle terrains encountered. However, it is important to note that specific situations might require different courses of action.

1. (a). Drink as much as you think you need before you begin to feel thirsty.

The danger in the situation is dehydration, and once the process begins, your limited water supply will not do much good in reversing it. Saving or rationing will not help, especially if you become unconscious due to dehydration or sunstroke. It is advisable to drink a little at a time before you become thirsty. So use the water as you feel you need to without wasting it and be aware of the necessity to find a water source as soon as possible.

2. (c). Drink some lightly salted water.

A large loss of body water and salt causes heat exhaustion. Drinking water mixed with a small amount of salt will help to replace electrolytes that have been lost due to dehydration. It is also important to get into the shade immediately and to lie down, preferably on something that is elevated above the ground. You want to avoid chocolate because it contains caffeine, which will cause a greater loss of fluids.

3. (a). Make a lot of noise.

Snakes do not like people and will usually do everything they can to get out of your way. Unless you surprise or corner a snake, there is a good chance that you will not even see one, let alone come in contact with it. Some snakes do feed at night, and walking softly may bring you right on top of one.

4. (c). Soak your arm in the mountain stream.

You need to cool the skin as rapidly as possible and for fifteen to thirty minutes to prevent further tissue damage. A cool, rushing mountain stream provides a perfect source to do this. Remove clothing and jewelry as soon as possible in case of swelling, but do not remove any clothing that is stuck to the burn. Clean the burn and apply a dry dressing, but do not apply any type of ointment, spray, or oil because this traps the heat inside the burn.

5. (b). Proceed with only your socks on.

Wearing only socks, you will be able to pick your route to some degree as you better feel where you are stepping. Normal hiking boots can become slippery, and going barefooted offers no protection to your feet.

6. (a). Put the batteries under your armpits to warm them, and then replace them in the flashlight.

Flashlight batteries lose much of their power, and weak batteries run down faster in the cold. Warming the batteries will restore them for a while. You should avoid night travel because there are too many obstacles that might injure you.

7. (c). Moon.

In the Southern Hemisphere, you would normally look for the Southern Cross constellation and adjacent pointer stars because the North Star is not visible from this latitude. However, northern Peru is close to the equator, so the Southern Cross is of limited use as it lies too low on the horizon. Therefore, the moon can be used to determine direction by observing which side is illuminated. If the moon rises before the sun has set, the lit side will be the west. If the moon rises after midnight, the lit side will be the east. That is to say, the illuminated side of the moon points toward the sun. This gives a rough east-west reference during the night.

8. (b). Yellow.

A yellow flame indicates incomplete combustion and that there is a strong possibility for the build-up of carbon monoxide. You should make sure that you have proper ventilation in the tent to prevent this from happening.

9. (c). Across the stream.

You will have the best stability facing across the stream and keeping your eye on the exit point on the opposite bank. The worst alternative would be to face upstream because the current could push you back, whereby anything like a pack would unbalance you and knock you down.

10. (b). No later than 4:00 in the afternoon.

It is important to set up camp in a jungle environment *at least* one hour prior to twilight because it becomes dark almost instantly. In April, the sun would set at approximately 5:30 p.m. in this part of Peru. Locating camp near a source of water would increase your exposure to mosquitoes and other insects. Also, it is never a good idea to settle down near the large trees located in the jungle, as poisonous ants, rodents, and other small animals find shelter in the numerous cavities around the base of such trees.

11. (a). Apply iodine.

The bite of a leech is usually painless, but the average leech can draw as much as two tablespoons of blood in under half an hour. To remove one, you can apply salt, iodine, lemon juice, vinegar, or insect repellent. You can use intense heat from a lighter or lit cigarette to remove a leech, but this can cause a severe burn. You should not remove a leech by pulling because it can leave the mouth parts in the wound, which can become infected.

12. (a). Fall flat on your back and float.

Quicksand is comprised of sand mixed with water. It is much denser than salt water so people can easily float in it. The problem is that quicksand acts like a vacuum and will suck you under if you increase movement. It is important to move as smoothly as possible; don't struggle, push, or pull. The way to survive is to cease quick fearful movements, float on your back, and simply relax. Then, using slow movements to reduce viscosity, you can paddle to safety. If carrying anything with you, drop it immediately and don't hold onto anything that will weigh you down.

INDIVIDUAL DECISIONS TALLY SHEET

Group	Average Individual Score	Highest Individual Score
Example	*7.3*	*9*
Group 1		
Group 2		
Group 3		
Group 4		
Group 5		
Group 6		
Average for all groups		

GROUP DECISIONS TALLY SHEET

Group	Score for Group Consensus	Gain/Loss Over Average Individual Score	Gain/Loss Lowest Individual Score	Synergy
Example	*10*	*+2.7*	*+1*	*Yes*
Group 1				
Group 2				
Group 3				
Group 4				
Group 5				
Group 6				
Average for all groups